The Other Side

KAT NAUD

Fulton Books
Meadville, PA

Published by Fulton Books 2021

ISBN 978-1-63710-848-2 (paperback)
ISBN 978-1-63710-849-9 (digital)

Printed in the United States of America

CHAPTER 1

How Everything Can Change in Thirty Seconds

You will never feel as free as when you are on the back of a horse. There is something indescribable about galloping through a field, just the two of you in unison. That's what cross-country is. You and your horse sharing one brain. So in sync that you can take on the world.

It's that kind of partnership that makes a great cross-country team. Full trust in each other—that's the feeling I had with Jackson.

Jackson and I spent a decade cultivating this connection, and it was all starting to paying off. With our sights set on one day, representing Canada at the Olympics, we headed out on course. Cross-country had always been my favorite and best phase. Getting to do it today on my twenty-fifth birthday felt like a dream come true.

Warm-up was all done, and he was feeling amazing. Ready to dominate! Time to head to the start box.

My horse eagerly danced below me; this was not his first "rodeo." There was nothing like a start-box countdown to get your heart rate pumping. Those two minutes in the box before you set out on course made time slow down—hyper-aware of every flex of muscle below me, the feeling of my saddle beneath my seat. Time stood still until a familiar place in the countdown snapped me back to reality.

"Five, four, three, two, one… Go!"

A deep breath, a kick, and on we were. Jackson was a cross-country machine. I didn't have to ask him twice. He shot out of the holding box like a rocket. The kind of gallop that would put most racehorses to shame.

There were a lot of horses out there that you have to rev up to the first few fences until the rhythm of the course sets in. Jackson was not one of those. From his first stride out, he was with me. People have often asked how we "make them" jump, but the truth is, there was no forcing this horse. He was just as eager as me to tear up the course.

With our first jump in our sight, it was time to balance. Jackson is an exceptionally large horse with a huge stride, so helping him to the right distance required some work. Most horses canter on a 12-foot long stride, but Jackson, being 17.3-foot hand high, and having a back that towered over my head, would easily stroll about in an 18-foot step. Adjusting myself back into the saddle and a few tugs against the reins, he shifted back over his hind legs in preparation. It is your job as the rider to see the distance you are riding. This way you can help your horse balance and make sure you arrive at the jump at the same time. The worst thing a rider could do is to get there too early. It not only throws yourself into a dangerous position, but it pushes your horse out of balance. They now, instead of just lifting their front end off the ground, have to push your body weight up as well.

Six strides out, and I knew we were right on step. We sailed over the large table like a bird taking flight, landed, and galloped onward to tackle the rest of the course.

Usually, a course designer sets the first few fences on course as "gallop fences," meaning they are easy to just roll up to and are designed to help get your rhythm and bearings out on the field.

By fence 4, the challenge was upped. A ninety-degree turn from table to table. A great first combination to make sure we were awake, focused, and on the aids. Jackson made quick work of it all. Having had him since he was a three years old and doing all his training myself, I knew all I had to do was to shift my balance back over my hips, steady his pace, and look in the direction of the second jump in the combination. He ate it up.

The rest of the course went just like that. Jackson and I in full unison feeding off each other's cues. As we approached the water, a question that makes many horses hesitate and look, I felt Jackson perk up. He was not like any horse I had ridden before. He was exactly like me, and sometimes that made me work a lot harder. A usual horse would see this large solid roll-top fence, standing at three-and-a-half feet tall and even wider than its height, and they would notice the water behind it that they were landing into and suck back, slow their step, and put a hesitant effort in. Many horses just clear the fence with the bare minimum to give themselves the extra few seconds to look and judge the obstacle. Jackson, on the other hand, was just like me, a total show-off. He saw this as a chance to strut his stuff—putting in a massive jump, clearing the fence by a good extra foot and a bit. The resulting extra power from his hind end sprung me up out of the tack and made me lose my stirrups.

We landed the jump, and there was no time to hesitate for three strides. Across the water was a large open corner fence shaped like a triangle. You had to jump the open point between two flags, only separated by a few feet, so accuracy was key. There was no time to hesitate or fuss over regaining my stirrups; we were going to have to go without. This large question was one of the harder points on course, but I trusted my partner explicitly. I knew all I had to do was get his attention to the right place, lift his balance back up, and he was taking me there.

He didn't let me down.

With the biggest challenge of the course behind us, everything else was smooth sailing. The rest of our course flew by in foot-perfect fences, with one fence left before heading toward home. I quickly glanced at my watch to check our time, and we were right on track. Thirty seconds to get over the last fence and cross the finish line. The cross-country phase was timed, and anything after the "optimum time" left a rider penalized per second over.

Cross-country was the third phase in this competition, and we were leading our division. After two amazing phases the day before, I was so excited to bring home the blue ribbon and add this to my list of qualifiers.

"It's funny how in just thirty seconds, your whole life can change."

Our last fence was a large upright table; nothing new or strange to any upper-level cross-country rider. A table is like filler, like adding bread to your dinner, it is not providing you with the same nutrients as your protein and veggies, but it's helping make up the full meal. Course designers throw these fences in to give the rider a chance to breathe or build confidence after a tough combination, or in this case, as a smooth easy finish to an otherwise challenging course.

I was already beaming with pride how our course had ridden, when I realized we were in trouble. We were four strides out, and we had four-and-a-half steps ahead. We were a whole six feet away from a good jumpable distance. That means there was a whole half a stride we had to make up, and make up quickly.

Cross-country jumps come up fast. The jumps are big and solid, and your reaction time can be the difference between a great story of a tough ride, or a complete disaster. Well, that's the kind of distance I was facing. I knew Jacksons' buttons, having trained them in myself. I knew that this massive horse would always prefer to lengthen his step and jump big and bold over having to shorten and compress. Without hesitation, I sat as tall as possible to keep my body weight out of his way. I kicked and urged him to make up the distance.

For the first time in our ten-year relationship, Jackson sucked back, slowed, and saw a completely different distance than me. We had always had the same eye for a big bold spot until today.

Jackson put in a tiny bunny-hop stride into the remaining six feet and tried his best to use every ounce of athletics in his body to get himself out. It was simply too tight; it wasn't enough space. His knees caught the front face of the table. There was no getting out of this unscathed.

We had been traveling 550 meters per minute or 33 kilometers per hour for those non-horsy readers until the fence caught his front end. The sheer momentum from his speed pushed his hind end up in the air as we began to flip. His hind end traveled first. We summersaulted into a rotational fall.

Rotational falls are the most dangerous type of fall a rider can have. We train and do our best to try to roll or get out of the way. Sometimes, like this time, there just wasn't room.

Jackson flipped over the fence, landing on his back, pinning me between him and the ground. The sheer force of his speed sent us sliding ten feet, with me still trapped beneath him. Five hundred fifty meters a minute to being landed on by my 1,300-pound horse.

Landing flat on my back beneath him, I couldn't breathe. The oxygen felt like it was gone from my lungs, and there was no space to regain it. Being pushed deeper into the earth by the weight of Jackson's large body, I gasped for air. I felt hyperaware that my head and neck were in line with the top of his back and shoulders. His legs flailed above my eyesight in shear panic. He was going to try to stand, and I was still going to be beneath his feet.

Horses have a natural instinct to get up. Being prey animals, they are ingrained with the desire to be able to flee when they feel threatened. Having just done an unnatural flip through the air, like an Olympic gymnast mid routine, this felt pretty threatening to him. Horses can't understand reason in those moments, just the urge to get back to feeling safe. Fight or flight.

As he flailed above me in an effort to regain his hooves to the ground, I saw his right front foot hit the ground, inches from my face. Then, in a flash, he was up. He had contorted himself like unwinding a pretzel to miss my body. For the first time, I could inhale. The weight finally removed; my lungs greedily gasped for more air. Having the wind knocked out of you at any time is an unsettling feeling, but having the wind physically crushed out of you is a whole other ball game.

I have always been trained to be "tough." You fall off a horse, you get back up. You get back on.

As I gasped, still fighting to breathe, I pushed away from the cold ground beneath me and tried to rise. The harder I pushed up against my elbows, the more I was aware of my body's resistance to move.

Our brain sends signals to our body, and it responds, but not today. As I collapsed back to the cold earth below me, I knew something was wrong. Never had I fallen and not been able to get back up. Having ridden my whole life, I was no stranger to tumbles or even significant falls. I had always risen despite the pain and injury. I laid on the ground, willing my body to move, and nothing came.

I couldn't turn my head to see but heard the sounds of rushing feet in my direction, and in a blink of an eye, was surrounded by people—my mom, the medical team, and the jump judge, who had been at my fence. The first-aid provider knelt above my head in an effort to stabilize my neck and prevent me from moving. I could hear the sound of my mother's frantic voice behind me but couldn't see her. She always keeps it together in moments of crisis; in fact, she is the person I would normally pick to be stuck in a scary situation with. I could tell by her tone how panicked she truly was.

As I lay there, at the total mercy of this stranger supporting my spine, all I could think was where is my horse. I began to panic. Had he been injured in the fall? Did he break his leg, or worse, his neck? I couldn't move or turn to look for him, so I began to cry. A frantic plea to the people in my surroundings to get me an update, any update so I knew he was okay.

Finally, after what felt like an eternity, my mom bent over beside me. For the first time, I could see her. All the color had drained from her face, and she looked as if she had seen a ghost. That's when I knew it was bad. My first thought went to Jackson didn't make it, and I began to sob. As I cried, I slowly became aware of my feet sliding back and forth frantically against the ground.

I lay on the ground for what felt like hours, when the sound of distant sirens began to ring out. I knew those alarms were ringing to come take me, but I couldn't go! How could they take me until I knew my horse was okay? Jackson was way more than my pet; he was my partner, my best friend, and I had no idea if he had survived this horrific fall, or if he was going to be okay.

Fighting against the hands holding me still, I thrashed around from side to side. I must have appeared like a fish out of water, wiggling aggressively around on the ground.

Finally, my mom, knowing I wasn't going to go quietly without at least an update, got ahold of one of the girls back at the stable.

Much to my relief, her pale complexion and worry was not over Jackson, it was about me. She informed me my working student, Michelle, who had been with me and Jackson since the beginning, had him. He was running back toward the barn when she caught up with him.

Michelle knew me so well; she was like the glue that helped hold our team together. She was the only one who could handle excited Jackson's post course, and she knew me like she was my little sister.

Putting aside her worry for me, she, somehow reading my mind, went right for the thing I cared for most, Jackson.

She and the rest of my team had him untacked, cooled down, iced, and at the vets. They all moved together like a well-oiled machine despite these being unprecedented circumstances for them all. Each one of the team jumped right to action like they had done this a million times. One girl on untacking, another on sponging the ice water on to cool him, while another followed with the sweat scraper to get the water back off. It is so important to get the cold water off right away, or it can actually turn hot from their body heat, and in turn, reheat the horse.

Jackson was fine; he would be a little stiff, but no injuries to be found.

I must have cushioned his landing.

With a relieved sigh, I calmed as the ambulance attendance strapped me onto a backboard and loaded me into the vehicle, with my mom nervously at my side.

CHAPTER 2

Aftermath

Everything from there was a blur, sliding in and out of awareness as the pain took hold. Bouncing around on a hard backboard through an uneven field felt like someone was playing a cruel joke on me. I couldn't take the jolting anymore. It was like bouncing up and down on a trampoline made of concrete. Just then, only minutes into our drive, we came to a stop, and I sighed with relief.

As they opened the back doors of the ambulance, I was blasted with loud sounds of air being pushed around. *Were we in a tornado?* I fought the urge to click my heels and utter, "There's no place like home," as if I was in the opening scene of *The Wizard of Oz*.

No, no tornado. I was being unloaded from the ambulance and loaded into a helicopter.

Now I have been lucky enough to have flown in a helicopter several times. I arrived to my high-school graduation in one, and I can honestly say without hesitation that this new flight was by far the least fun.

My head held straight by a neck brace; my body strapped to a hardboard. They began to pump me with pain medicine. I deliriously attempted to argue, but all my efforts were thwarted. I was too concussed and in too much shock to explain I'm a cheap drunk when it comes to pain medications, something I inherited from my mother.

Ten minutes into our amazing aviation experience, and I began to show them why I don't take meds. I began to be sick! Not delicate ladylike sick, like in the movies when the girl is "cute ill," just a little green, where the leading man swoops her up and wants to care for her, but projectile vomiting still attached to the backboard. The closest comparison I could give you is a scene from the end of the exorcist, when the main character expelled the demon from her body.

Now I don't know if you have ever been lucky enough to throw up while strapped still, but it's impossible. Just the sheer motion of throwing up is usually a whole body experience, but not today. I was stuck in place, motionless like a corpse. There was nowhere for it to go. They couldn't turn me as the movement would sway the chopper and risk the safety of all the passengers on board, so I began to aspirate, choking and gasping for air. The scene around me began to go in and out.

It felt as though someone kept turning the lights off and on, and my eyes didn't have time to adjust.

I looked up helplessly at the air-ambulance attendant as she did her best to help clear my airway. I could see such pity on her face as she wiped away a tear from her eye.

Great. I was so pathetic. I was making strangers cry. Hashtag winning, not exactly the birthday celebration I had envisioned for myself.

The chopper ride seemed to go on and on, still unable to breathe through the contents of my stomach I had emptied across my face.

I have never, to date, know such relief as when the helicopter finally landed. That was the first time my ambulance attendant was able to turn me and fully clear my airway. As the team unloaded me and wheeled me into the hospital, all I could focus on was the ability to breathe. Twice today that liberty had been unwillingly taken away from me, and boy, did I ever appreciate having it back? It is such a basic thing, to breathe. We don't have to think about it. Even brand-new babies born know how. We take it for granted until it's taken away from us.

The whole accident and trip had happened in a matter of hours, but it had played out in slow motion. Now, being drugged and at the hospital, the next few days went by in fast forward.

Within minutes of arriving, I was in a bed and wheeled down to x-ray, CT, and MRI.

Being Canadian, I'm used to our "free" health-care system. We are over-run; the staff are overworked, and the hospitals are overfull. You wait forever to be seen, but not in the states. I guess you do really get what you pay for.

I had all my tests and results within an hour. A time that would have been unheard of back home. In a drug-induced fog, they pronounced me with a broken back. I broke my L2, L3, and L4 vertebrae. The sheer pressure of Jackson's body through my inflated air vest, a relatively new piece of safety equipment, actually broken the wings (transverse processes), clean off both sides of all three vertebrae.

I had been extremely lucky, I was told. They were convinced I would have severe internal crushed injuries and much more significant damage. Although a broken back is never a good thing, it was nothing compared to how bad it could have been. Rotational falls have an alarming rate of mortality because you are being compressed under a thousand-plus pounds.

Every doctor that saw me agreed my air vest had truly saved my life.

An air vest clips to your saddle and goes onto your body like a big vest. If, when you separate from your horse, it expands like an airbag in all directions around your torso and neck.

Taking a minute to process all the information the doctors game me, all I could think was this five-hundred-dollar investment had saved my life. I had been competing at the highest level at that competition and was the only person in warm-up wearing one.

I often hear people complain it's because of the cost, but the cost of one show had just saved my life. A worthwhile investment I would say.

*****

Days went by, and I was finally sprung from what felt like my own personal jail. We had been helicoptered to Seattle, so we had no car and no ride home. One of our amazing barn family dads had driven our fifty-six-foot truck and trailer filled to the brim with dogs, equipment, and all the team horses back home, but that still left us renting a car to make the trip back.

Leaving the hospital was the first time postfall I had stood. I had been made to sit up a few times, but fully weight baring and having to pivot into the car was excruciating. The pressure of my body made my spine felt like it was going to collapse. As I slid into the SUV we had rented, I gasped at the motion. I had spent days on pain meds, and this was the first time I got to take real stock of how my body felt. It wasn't good. All my pain seemed to be middle to lower back, and somehow a bit worse on the left. When my left hip made contact with the soft fabric of the car seat, it was as if I was sitting against cement.

Our car ride was a short hour and a half, but every bump sent a rattle through my spine. It was like playing the xylophone up my backbones as you would see in a children's Halloween show on a dancing skeleton.

Every breath, shift, and bump was pain. It was a level of pain I had truly never experienced before.

Finally, we made it. I have never been so relieved to be back at the barn. Fighting against my mom's protest, I broke free of the car and shuffled my way into the barn.

I had to see him, assess him with my own eyes to believe he was okay. As I pushed the big metal barn doors apart, a familiar nicker greeted me.

We have fifty-six horses, with over two hundred people through our barn every week, but that horse recognized me in an instant. He seemed as relieved as I to lay eyes on each other. We had never had a fall and then not gotten right back on, let alone not see each other for days.

We embraced each other in silence. A long slow hug. No words between this majestic animal and I were needed to describe the relief we both felt.

Using his large chest to lean against, I stood there for so long, taking some of the pressure off my crippling back pain.

Finally, my mom, being able to stay patient no longer, broke up our embrace. It had been one hell of a five-day stint for her as well, and she was terrified that one knock from Jackson's head, and I would be on the floor.

Normally, after a competition, I would be unpacking, wrapping Jackson, and en route to my own apartment, but not today. Still showing concussion symptoms and being too weak to get up and down by myself, I was grounded to my parent's house. My fall had happened on a Sunday, and it was now Wednesday. I had at least a week left of digressing back to teenage, living at home life.

The next two days were dull. Full of long naps and boring daytime television. When Friday finally rolled around, I was excited for the physical challenge the weekend held.

That weekend was Campbell Valley Horse Trials, a show I had committed to taking students to at the start of the year. I had eight kids competing, and

I knew they would all drop out if I couldn't come. Being the stubborn Leo I am, I knew I could make it.

A three-day event involves hours of standing, horse holding, and course walking. Something that in my current physical state seemed like climbing Everest. Luckily, one of my fellow riders and great friends came up with a brilliant solution of having my students film their course walk. That way, I could still coach and not have to walk upward of ten kilometers. The weekend was filled with long days and a ton of pain, probably too much for a freshly broken back, but I filled it with pride for my students. Having not missed a Campbell Valley event in almost two decades, I wasn't about to start now.

Being back at a show also got me excited about getting back in the tack myself.

I was told a few months off I would be good as new. As hard as it was to stay off my horse, at least I got to still be involved in my sport, and there would still be some season left for me before the winter weather hit and the 2015 season was done.

Having to miss two months of competing when you have a big audacious goal, like Olympics, was for sure a setback, but we still had time. It made sense not to rush it and to, probably for the first time in my life, listen to my doctor and be patient.

CHAPTER 3

The Best Laid Plans

Those months of healing dragged on. Every day, out at the barn teaching, I was bitter. Having to walk past my beautiful prince of a horse and yet not permitted to throw caution to the wind and tack up was torture.

Sweet relief finally came on a Monday morning. Three months exactly since my fall, and I couldn't wait another second. Having had the life scared out of her, my mother insisted upon being there for the first ride back, in case Jackson was feeling his oats and the time off.

I was already tacked and standing on the mounting block when she finally strolled into the arena.

"You're late," I snapped. I was letting my impatience get the better of me. It was only five minutes, but I couldn't wait another second. She rolled her eyes and walked over to hold Jackson's reins as I mounted.

As my hips met the saddle and found the familiar grooves of my tack, I couldn't help thinking it was like putting on a pair of well-broken shoes—a perfect fit.

As I softened my hips and gave a gentle squeeze of my leg, tears began to roll down my cheek. At first, it was a feeling of relief that I was finally back on top of the horse that made me feel whole. Jackson and I were like two pieces of a puzzle. The picture wasn't fully complete without the other half.

But as I took a contact on the reins and a deep breath, I realized the tears were a warning.

I had always had athlete mode turned on when on the back of a horse. I never seemed to notice the world around me, and I didn't feel pain. I have actually fallen, resulting in a broken nose, at ten, and not shed a tear, and continued on with my lesson. That sort of focus had allowed me to tune out what was happening around me, allowed me to focus on my horse, but that "skill" often masked other things…but not today.

The longer we walked, the harder it became. Ever step felt like my spine could shatter into a million pieces. Just the sheer motion of this horse's long elegant stride sent me into a tailspin of pain.

Trying to wipe any evidence of struggle from my face, in an attempt not to be discovered, I gathered my rains even shorter and pressed for a trot.

I refused to still be injured. How could I? I need more time! I just needed to find my inner strength, suck it up, and keep going. After all, I had never broken my back before; this must be normal for getting back into the swing of things.

The longer we trotted, the more I knew. A deep pit in my stomach confirmed what I was already feeling throughout my body. I was not okay. As I pulled the leather of my remains back toward my body, I collapsed over my hands. Anything to unweight my body from the seat of my saddle.

I got off in total defeat. Have you ever had a dream ripped away? Goals totally crushed? Well, that was what was happening in front of my eyes, and there was nothing I could do to stop it.

CHAPTER 4

Time Doesn't Heal All Wounds

Having taken all my required time off and still struggling with the pain, I started to look elsewhere for some healing aids. I started with massage therapy. Having biweekly massages always felt amazing, but it was providing me more with a Band-Aid. Don't get me wrong, it helped, but more in the day-to-day survival.

Next, I added IMS (intermuscular stimulation) which, to explain simply, is physio, putting needles into your muscles and attaching them to a low-grade electrical current that stimulates spasms. The idea behind it was to create activity within the muscle and encourage it to start working normally again. It was a bit like torture, especially, when after months, it hadn't helped.

Months of that abuse, with little to no progress, and I had to stop. Who likes feeling electrocuted weekly, especially when it wasn't even working? This led me to chiropractic.

Through the chiropractor and new patient x-rays, I learned that a few things had been missed on my diagnosis. Firstly, knowing nothing about human anatomy, I had always assumed your L2 to L4 were lower down as that's where the bulk of my pain was. When in fact, they are in the very middle of your back. Clearly, my knowledge of horse anatomy hadn't carried over to humans.

We also learned that not only was my pelvis currently dislocated, but I also had a fracture on the bottom left side of my pelvis. No wonder I was still in so much pain.

Having no desire to "rock the boat" with my currently disassembled body, the chiropractor sent me with a copy of my x-rays to my doctor's office.

I have been lucky enough to have had the same doctor since I was a baby. Everyone I know struggles to find a decent family physician. When I walked into the office, white as a ghost, no appointment on the books, they fit me in.

One look at my imagination, and my doctor agreed. My injuries could have been operable at the time, but being months after the fact, it was too late. He relocated my pelvis, which let me tell you is the most ungodly pain you have ever experienced. A hollow bone-shattering crack that made your stomach turn and your toes curl all at the same time.

My healing time was extended, and I was devastated. I knew that this time off was going to take any chance of the Olympics off the table.

The only plus side was my pelvis was finally rehomed in its socket. Standing and weight-bearing was instantly so much easier.

Instead of the pity party, I threw myself into work. I taught as much as I could and slowly started to craft a plan B. Okay, yes, this Olympics was off the table, but there would be more. Jackson and I were young, and we had time. It was time to lean into what it did best—planning.

Six months off, and another four for rehab, and we could be in prime, placing to run for 2020. Nothing like a back-up plan to reinspire. I have always been the type who needs a goal. Something to chase, something that excites me and inspires me to get out of bed every morning. It is just who I am. I would be lost without that drive.

Having to learn to take the sidelines were a role I was not altogether comfortable with. If a student's horse was tough, or a client was away, all I wanted to was volunteer my services, throw my foot in the stirrups, and get to work. Being "benched" was like being punished for a crime I didn't commit. Every show became torture. Helping people achieve their goals all from the sidelines was so foreign. Don't get me wrong, my students are my pride and joy; every success they had made my heart gush, but I was used to running alongside them. Now I was just the chick in charge from the ground.

Show season finally came to a complete as we wrapped up the last event and prepared for winter. Winter season is for riders to do their homework. Time to get back to the basics, put in the work, and start building your skills for next season. There is no more sacrificing every weekend on the road all across North America, and I was looking forward to the downtime. A little let off from the pressure of the constant *go, go, go* that came with the summer and fall months. I had also been nagged for months about slowing down my schedule to give my back and pelvis a true chance to rest. More days off with my feet up and no pressure.

CHAPTER 5

The Day Hope Died

Rest, how exciting. Time to catch up on your favorite Netflix series or binge-watch friends for the umpteenth time, or not. Rest is only exciting for the first forty-eight hours, then you're left with the crippling boredom, stiff useless body, and the urge to break out of your home and run through a field of flowers, like Julie Andrews, in *The Sound of Music*. I figured while being off, I would at least be getting progressively better, but the opposite seemed to be true. Every resting day, I seemed tighter. Every week, the pain seemed to escalate, and every month, it became harder and harder to bear.

Going on rest is something, looking back, that I can say with complete confidence, was the worse decision I ever made. Succumbing to the doctor's recommended light-duty living was the biggest step backward in my healing. When you get up each day with a goal, or a big work project (for me a show), it's something driving you forward. Something that keeps you moving one step at a time. And although the logic behind physical rest at the time seemed like sound advice, it took me back to as bad, if not worse, than I was right after the accident.

I had been surviving on motion and drive, but having those gone, my body seized, started to lock up and stiffen.

One day, my left foot started to go numb. Now when people hear the word "numb," they assume lack of feeling. It is just not the case. Numbness is like an unholy pain that burns through your skin as if you accidentally put your foot in lava. Think pins and needles and steroids. Unfortunately for me, this "numbness" was accompanied by a change in skin color and temperature.

The final straw was losing the ability to flex my toes. That was it. I had to go in and find out why I was slowly digressing.

Now I know what you're thinking: How could I wait for it to get to that point before caving and going into the doctor's office? I had been in there so many times. With my injuries, I felt like I should start collecting frequent flyer miles or have my own room dedicated to me. So for this reason, I had put it off. Losing the ability to move your foot altogether was the push-over-the-edge to suck it up and go in.

After five minutes of being examined, my doctor looked at me with a panicked look clearly displayed across his face, and said, "I think you're getting back surgery today, kid."

He was concerned that the broken wings off my vertebrae (transverse processes) had shifted and were now interfering with my spinal cord, and I was risking paralysis. He wrote me a requisition and sent me downtown to our spinal specialty hospital.

I am pretty sure that's the fastest any human has made it from Langley, British Columbia, to Vancouver, the normal hour drive zoomed by in thirty minutes flat.

I parked the car in the emergency lot, limped my way in, and handed the triage nurse behind the counter my requisition.

Now I figured with a doctor's note would get me amazing care, but the opposite seemed to be true.

I waited for hours. I waited for hours, terrified. Terrified that every shift in my chair, every trip to the bathroom or sneeze, could paralyze me. Finally, after what felt like an eternity, they called my name. I have never been so excited or eager to see a doctor in my life. I leaped up from my chair, forgetting my anxiety of over moving, and followed a nurse to an exam room.

After an additional ten minutes of waiting, a doctor finally appeared from behind the pale-blue curtain. He walked in, sat down, and I handed him the requisition from my doctor.

He put it down. He didn't even glance at the paper. This doctor asked me one question, why was I there? Frustrated, as it is all in the note, I explained my doctor's concerns and said I was hoping for imaging to confirm his frightening diagnosis.

Now this man, who I had waited over four hours to see, didn't examine me; he didn't question me any further, didn't ask me about my pain or order a single test. He looked at me, and said, "What drugs do you want?"

Startled, as I don't believe in taking opioids for chronic pain, I believe it to be one of the largest causes of addiction, I quickly assured him I was there for help, not drugs. He responded frankly, "Well, I'm busy, so you can take the drugs, or you can leave." So I left.

My parting words as I walked away were, "Do you remember when you became a doctor to help people?" See what I mean about our Canadian health-care system, you get what you pay for.

That was a moment I will never forget.

That's was the exact moment for me that hope died. I had always stayed positive throughout this pain journey until now. That doctor and his complete lack of care stripped me of any hope, for how could I stay positive when the very person whose job is to help me couldn't even be bothered?

Things got dark from here.

Depression started to kick in. Many doctors told me my injuries were permanent, but I had always refused to believe them until now.

Still terrified of the prospect of my vertebrae interfering, I finally got x-rays. Thankfully, that diagnosis was disputed, and a new one took its place.

Complex regional pain syndrome—which is a fancy way to say I had crushed the nerves in my back, and it was creating pain in my foot from the damage—I was prescribed gabapentin, a drug that blocked the neuro receptors in your brain to trick your mind out of feeling the pain.

This drug was a horrific for me. It allowed me to feel a 10 percent relief to the burning and numbness, but it came at a price. That price was my body. One of the most common side effects is weight gain. I was unfortunately one recipient to get this, and in a big way. By my third month on the drug, I had gained thirty pounds.

Not only did I no longer recognize my body, having always been a fit and a healthy athlete, but there was much more weight adding pressure to my injuries. Every five pounds added felt like a million more on my back. The more pain added, the harder it was to keep moving. The harder it was to move, the more weight came. It was like being in a washing machine. Each turn over, pushing the next one further.

Every day I went further in the wrong direction until I couldn't take it anymore.

My life, once so full of promise and ambition, became a dark hole. Nothing but broken dreams and pain to accompany me. Battling depression is not something I wish upon anyone. Each day, the fog of darkness creeps a little further over your subconscious until it completely distorts your reality. Have you ever seen the movie *The Fog*? Well, it's like that, a dark thick fog, covering all that was once good or happy and leaving you stumbling around in the dark, looking for a flashlight.

CHAPTER 6

From Victim to Survivor

That emergency-room doctor can never really know that those five minutes we spent together was the beginning of my breaking point. That those five minutes and his lack of care was my final straw. It was the last piece of my hope, and my sanity was cracking.

It was the start of my bottom. Every last piece of what made up my personality slowly started to slip away. I began missing work, withdrawing from people I cared about. The idea of going out and being my once-social self seemed impossible. Who would want to go out and be with the now "Michelin man" version of them self-limping through the restaurant? Not me.

I also couldn't stand the pity anymore. The sheer look on my friends faces as they watched me hobble around. I couldn't stand the "see-you-shouldn't-ride" talks, or even worse the "everything-happens-for-a-reason" speeches. I have come to see and realize now it's the last thing someone struggling wants to hear.

Even getting out of bed in the morning became a chore. Don't get me wrong; it had always hurt to get up, but there was always something to get moving for. Now that hope was gone and my drive and goals were ripped away, I started to lose my battle with depression.

I had been fighting it off for so long, but I just couldn't justify it anymore. When you are twenty-five years old and you have more days ahead of you than behind you and you spend every day hitting a ten out of ten in pain, with no end in sight, that's hard to accept. When every doctor says your injuries are permanent and you will not recover, how do you sign up for that being your reality?

I didn't know anymore!

My rock bottom came on a Wednesday. I have had a fight with someone, and I was out of spoons.

Now, if you have never heard the spoon theory, it's made by a woman named Christine Miserandino. She created a fabulous way to understand life in chronic pain because it's a hard and lonely venture. Friends and family don't understand. You are also thankful they don't understand as it means they don't suffer the way you do, but it means you're alone in the journey. Pain is so hard to perceive. It's not something you can see; it's something you feel, and no one can really feel it for you. You cannot show it to anyone.

People understand pain with a broken arm with a cast, or a sprained ankle with a brace, something they can see. But pain is so much more than that. Pain comes from so many ways that it is impossible, as an outsider looking in, to know what someone is battling behind the closed doors of their body. Pain, whether it be physical or mental, is all encompassing and makes even the small daily tasks feel like climbing Everest.

That's why the spoon theory was a revelation for people like me, struggling to communicate the pain I was really facing.

Christine describes pain as waking up every morning with a number of spoons. Each daily task takes a spoon from you, and when you are out of spoons, you are out.

So for example, say, you get ten spoons a day, sounds like enough, doesn't it?

What people not in pain do not realize is waking up and getting out of bed, that's a spoon. Getting dressed and brushing your teeth, that is a spoon. Making breakfast, that is a spoon. God forbid you have to shower that morning because that is, for sure, a spoon. Soon you are halfway through your spoons for the day, and you haven't even left your house. Even the smallest daily tasks take a spoon from you.

Well, that particular day, I was out of spoons. I was out of spoons when someone unloaded their day on me. Now, normally, this would be water off a duck's back, but when you're in pain, your threshold to deal with any external pressures is so low that one little snip or a bad night sleep or upsetting news can send you into a complete tailspin of emotions.

That morning was a combination of all three. A perfect storm, if you will. I was done! All the pressure of living this way, pressure of where I saw my life at this point, the emotion of what I had lost—both physically and athletically—all came crushing down. I was done!

I laid on the floor of my bathroom, where I had fallen from my pelvis dislocations, yet again. I laid there for hours, stranded like a turtle that had been flipped on its back. Try as I might, I couldn't seem to convince my body to stand, so finally, I gave up.

Succumbing to my depression, I collapsed back against the cold shelf of the bathroom. I was holding a bottle of pain killers. A bottle that was completely full as I had always refused to take them, for fear of this exact outcome. The irony wasn't lost on me as I decided it was time. I could suffer no more. I needed to find peace.

As I slowly twisted off the childproof cap and poured the content of the small orange container into my hand, I began to weep. Tears flooding my eyes and falling to my lap at the thought of all the things I would miss and all the people I was leaving behind. It was the kind of "ugly cry" Dane Cook would describe, where you don't even try to wipe your eyes. You don't bother catching the tears as there was no way to catch up with the multitude streaking down my face.

That flood of emotions was interrupted by a small scratch at the bathroom door. It broke me out of my trance and brought me back down to reality. What would happen to that small little puppy on the other side if I went through with this today? Who would let her out? How long would she be left waiting till someone came? I put the pills back into the container and slid along the floor on my backside to open the door.

I let her in, and within a second, my seven-pound dog was on top of me. Her back feet standing on my lap, and her front paws resting on my shoulders. She looked me dead in the eyes as if seeing right into my soul. She stared me down, somehow knowing the decision I was struggling with! A wave of feelings came through me. It was like a silent communication I have never experienced before. A feeling that she knew I was struggling but she needed me, and she knew I could do this. We sat like that for five minutes, completely still, until I knew I had to be stronger. I knew I could push through this. This is why

I will always recommend a dog. They truly are man's best friend, and although I had rescued her from a kill shelter two years before, that day, she truly rescued me. I can say with full confidence, those four little paws, that scruffy hair, and her sweet soul saved my life.

The second my mindset changed, our eye contact was broken, and I was flooded with her little tongue, kissing me frantically. Licking all the tears away from my face in a somewhat aggressive manner, then turned my tears into hysterical laughter.

Now, all that was left was for me to stop the pity party, rise, and start the next phase of my life. I stretched my arms up high, grasped the edge of the cold round sink, and used every ounce of my upper-body strength I had to erect my body back to a stand. It took three tries and a lot of gasping through pain, but I was up. I stood there, still facing my bathroom mirror. I stared myself down, eye to eye, with the shadow self in the mirror, until finally, I bellowed out a cry. I yelled, and I mean literally yelled, "ENOUGH!" It was a battle cry. I needed to remind myself how strong I was, to remind myself of my inner strength. In that moment, I was flooded with all the skills I learned from riding. Now, I don't mean the physical skills or techniques, but the tough, stubborn, fight-back attitude it takes to be a professional athlete. No one ever got to tell me what kind of rider I could be, or what I could achieve with some grit and hard work, and this was no different. No one could say I couldn't recover, not even a doctor got to tell me that this was what the rest of my life would look like. The only person who could decide that was staring back at me in the glass, and she have had enough of this weak mental state.

I was done with "the victim," and I had to figure out how to become the survivor. It was time to take the first step, literally.

Tony Robbins describes changing your mood in two ways, by changing your focus and your physiology, and that's just what I had to do. I had to get moving. I started walking—five mandatory minutes a day of walking. I would leash my dogs up and hobble down the road like someone's ninety-year-old grandmother. Each walk felt like torture! That five minutes was the equivalent of running a marathon, but I kept at it. Weeks went by, and then the strangest thing happened. My walks started to get longer and faster. Then that thing that was torturing me every day became the thing that was getting me out of bed each day. It became the little time I carved out each day just for me. Being competitive, I started to challenge myself to go further and further, and that gave me back a little piece of myself I had lost. The goal-orientated, type-A personality, who needed to be challenged, who thrived off self-competition. It made me realize that as soon as I brought something into my day that brought me even the slightest amount of joy, life became worth living again. If all you have in your day is pain, that's a pretty sad existence, so having my little daily challenge and time with my fur babies inspired me that I could and I would survive this! It was the first time I felt like I had my brain back on my side.

Being physically strong through chronic pain is amazing, but what I had never known, previous to this experience, was that being mentally strong was going to be far more important. I had battled the pain for so long successfully until I lost the mental strength, and that is exactly what I had to start working on daily to get myself back to where I wanted to be.

CHAPTER 7

Saying Goodbye

Now, all of this movement was doing wonders in uplifting my mood and regaining my body I had once knew. But there was still a large part of healing left. That was the emotional side. I needed to accept the loss, grieve it, and forgive myself.

I needed to let myself off the hook and forgive my body for not being able to recover. You are always told growing up that when you are young, you heal so much better than when you're older, and yet my body had failed me. I had accepted that these physical changes were going to keep me from returning to my Olympic aspirations, and that was okay. Just because I had spent the better part of two decades chasing a dream I would never achieve doesn't mean that those years were wasted. It didn't mean that I was a failure. Those years molded me into the tough, strong, independent woman I had become today. That those years had been cultivating an inner strength that had allowed me to survive the challenges ahead of living in pain. That those years were what was going to make me successful in whatever avenue I decided to pursue.

Now these realizations didn't come easy; they were filled with tons of self-reflection, a lot of tears and grieving and, if I'm honest, some Sauvignon Blanc.

Accepting that my upper-level eventing career was over also came at a price. I couldn't be selfish and squander the talents of Jackson. Just because I would never be physically able of achieving our dreams we had worked so hard at didn't mean his journey was over.

My beautiful, athletic partner still had so much talent left in him. Just standing still, he looked like a future Olympian, and I couldn't take that away from him. He was too good and too in love with cross-country for me to be that selfish.

I made the heart-wrenching decision of letting him go. This horse, who was a piece of my soul, needed to go on without me and achieve the greatness I had planned up for the both of us.

Deciding to break my own heart was one thing, but actually putting it into action was another completely different story. Weeks went by as I procrastinated. Being a total type-A personality, that's something generally I'm not comfortable with, but I couldn't help it. I had to find the perfect situation for him. No one seemed good enough, and no barn or rider seemed worthy of his amazing athleticism. Finally, a riding friend and coach, who had heard through the grapevine I was considering letting him go back to competing without me, reached out. We had ridden and coached together for years, always seeing each other at the familiar shows. Her daughter's upper-level horse had come up lame (meaning sore or limping for the non-horse readers), and she was looking for something to play with. She was the opposite of Jackson and I. He was a horse with no rider. Hesitantly, I agreed for him to be her new mount and head across the border to their farm to get back to competing and ready to be sold.

The day, Jackson left to go to Oregon; my heart shattered as I watched the trailer pull out the drive and down the road. It was like the scene from *Flicka*, where her horse left and she chased the trailer all the way down the street, while it spontaneously went from sunny to rain, right in time with her emotions.

Well, I did not quite get the cooperation from Mother Nature to express my devastation, but the pain inside was enough to make it rain in my heart.

The first week without the presence of my best friend were spent sappy and pathetic. I was the love-scorned girl from the chick flick, lying on her bed. looking at his photo, and crying, "cue sappy chick flick music here." There was an emptiness that couldn't be filled. No amount of Ben and Jerry's peanut butter cup ice cream could fill the hole in my heart that Jackson left. I was always told, as a rider, no boy will ever break your heart because horses will prepare you for it. Truer words have never been spoken.

After a short few months of competing, Jackson caught the eye of an ambitious young rider named Brianna. She was looking for her four-legged Prince

Charming, and Jackson seemed to be a perfect fit.

The day of his vet check, having not seen him in five months, I drove the five hours down to be there, knowing this could very well be the last time I would see him again. Brianna lived in California, and if all went well today, he would be on a trailer within the week, heading to his new home.

That five-hour drive was a whirlwind of emotions—excited to see the love of my life again after months apart, terrified that he could pass his vetting and he would no longer be mine, and excited for him about the prospect of him getting his life back on track.

When I pulled into the long driveway of the farm, my breath stopped in my lungs. My beautiful prince was being ridden by this girl. A bubble of jealousy rose up in the back of my throat as I fought the urge to be sick. I could feel myself turning green with envy, like Bruce Banner fighting back the hulk inside. As I pulled my black car into the row of other cars parked along the front side of the red barn, I put it in park and just sat. I was frozen. I willed my legs to move or my arm to turn and open the door, but nothing came. The ache in my chest was what I imagine having a heart attack would feel like. Thoughts swirled through my head. Anger, followed by sadness, with a pinch of panic as the little voice in my head asked if I could actually have a stroke from being this devastated. As I sat, stationary, I watched—watched this beautiful girl, with auburn-red hair trailing behind her, float around the ring on Jackson. Realizing I could take no more, I put my car in reverse. This was a mistake. I shouldn't have come for this. I am not strong enough to say goodbye and have to sit with a pleasant smile, while someone steals my boy. I was just re-buckling my belt when they went over their first jump of the day together. I froze again, but not in the same way.

Jackson was an expressive and big jumper, and as the rider, you had to work hard to keep your own balance to not get in his way and not catch him in the mouth in an effort to use the bridle for your balance. Brianna did none of those. They fit together like puzzle pieces; the same way we once had. My big goofy guy threw and little squeal and leap on landing from a big oxer, showing how much he was truly enjoying himself. Instead of getting tense and pulling to overpower him, she laughed and pat his long muscular neck. That's when I knew. I knew they would make an amazing team, and I had to do this for him. This horse had done so much for me over the past eleven years. I owed him this much.

The little green monster I had turned into upon arrival was gone. It changed into pride. Pride over the majestic athlete that cantered in front of me. I had built that. I got to be the first half of his story, and she would be the second.

As she untacked, I slowly worked up the courage to introduce myself. She was delightful and sweet, everything I could have dreamt up for him. Damn it! I had so badly wanted not to like her.

We exchanged pleasantries and chatted about her few previous rides on Jackson. I could hear in her voice how excited she was. As she gushed over every detail, I was reminded of a schoolgirl in love. Exactly what he deserved.

The vet truck loudly pulled in the drive, and everyone went silent. She must have been as nervous as I was because our silence and pale expressions were in sync. As the clanging of metal equipment and bottles of medicine bounced around in the back, the vet truck rumbled up to the barn. An abrupt stop and the sound of heavy closing doors met our ears. She tentatively threw the halter over Jackson's large black head and led him to greet the vet that would decide all our fates today.

As the vetting began, I hovered quietly in the corner, anxiously waiting for the outcome. I was torn in two. Half of me praying he would pass his vetting and get to partner with his "new person" and half greedily praying he would fail and get to come home to me.

The vetting went on for hours. Being an expensive competition horse, nothing was left to chance. From flexions to check his joints, to looking in his eyes all the way to x-rays, no hair was left uncombed.

After an extensive vetting and what felt like days passing, he passed his check with flying colors. I was thrilled. As a horse seller previously, you are always relieved when a horse's vetting goes well, because as any horse person can tell you, anything can come up in the vet check. Than a slow realization crept over me that this was it, the last time I would see my partner. We had spent a decade growing together, and I had to say goodbye.

I slunk over to him, like a dog that had just been beaten, with all but my tail between my legs in defeat. This had been what I wanted so badly for him to find, but it was still going to be the thing that ripped me apart from the inside out. A long silent hug against his broad chest, a kiss, and the fastest good-bye I could get out to everyone, and I was back in my car. I just made it into the driver's seat as the tears came tumbling down.

It was a loss I can't even truly put to words. Half of my heart was gone, and I was never getting it back.

That five-hour drive home was silent; the only sound breaking through was me gasping for air between sobs. I wept the whole way from Oregon to the Canadian border. It is, to date, the hardest and longest I have ever cried for in my life. I must have looked such a fright as I pulled into the border stop. Some girls can pull off pretty cry. I would have even settled for mildly unattractive looking crier, but no, I look like a basset hound when I cry. My face somehow seemed to grow two inches outward in swelling, my cheeks became lobster red, and my eyes puffed up till where they look like a puffer fish. Thankfully, my eyes got even brighter blue, or you may miss them altogether through the inflammation.

As I rolled down my window, a blast of fall air met my cheeks, and they stung against the acidic burning my tears had left behind.

The large stern-looking man looking back at me from the tall booth in his lane looked at a loss for words. Normally, they give you a hard time, drill you about where you have been or items your bringing back, but not today. This beast of a man, who I'm sure was hired for his visual intimidation factors alone, looked down on me with such pity. He glanced at the cover of my navy-blue Canadian passport and uttered so softly, in a way that almost didn't seem to fit his size, "Please get home safely."

Knowing that if Jackson passed his vetting today, the tears wouldn't stop, I scheduled hosting a friend's going-away party to force myself to pull it together. I needed to dry my eyes and have a much-needed distraction from the emotional turmoil I felt inside. Jackson's vetting has taken so long I didn't have time to go home and change. I had spent the whole day at their farm and on the road, and I now had to go directly to the restaurant. The function was at a cute trendy pub. Luckily, I had some spare clothes in my car. As I pulled together the odds and ends of the "wardrobe" off the floor of my back seat, I cursed myself for my scheduling sabotage. All I wanted was to wallow in my flannel PJs, shut out the world, and perhaps some pepperoni pizza.

Sigh, I was already here. I had better pull it together and get in there. I changed in my car into the hodgepodge of clothes I had that didn't smell like horses and jumped out of my car, sadly not the first time I have done a wardrobe switch in the parking lot. I pulled a forced smile to my face, pulled the heavy oak door open, and moved on.

CHAPTER 8

Finding Your Identity

Nothing felt normal now. My mornings, usually consumed with thoughts of ponies and shows, now had an empty space. I swear I was like a little kid on Christmas every morning, with thoughts of sugar-plum fairies dancing in my head, but my fairies had four legs and hooves.

I didn't know how to fill my time. There was a void and a heart hurt that no amount of Netflix bingeing could cover. So I picked up a book, something most horse girls never have a spare minute to do unless they are on a beach in Mexico holding some fun umbrella drink in their hand, while simultaneously working on evening out their awkward rider tan lines.

I read cheesy romance books. I fell into the rabbit hole of teen vampire novels. I now clearly know I'm team Edward, important life information. But then a friend recommended "Rachel Hollis" to me. A writer and speaker who was just becoming well known. She gifted me a book that would forever change my life, *Girl, Wash Your Face!*

I looked at the title and though this doesn't seem like my jam, I mean, a book about washing your face? With a plethora of extra time and nothing left in the Hunger Games or Fifty Shades trilogies, I shrugged and gave it a chance.

That little book blew my mind. From the very first chapter, all the way to the last page, I lost time. I lost time in a way that hadn't happened to me off the back of a horse. Every word carefully thought out, seemed as if Rachel was writing it just for me.

Had she been secretly stalking me and wrote on that perspective? Should the title have switched to "Kat, Wash Your Face?"

For the first time in over a year, I felt inspired. I felt ready to believe in the little voice in the back of my head about where the next chapter of my life was going to come from. I found my courage and my voice.

That book inspired me to start my blog—a blog about life in chronic pain—and I called it The Other Side. What is "the other side" of chronic pain? I sure didn't know yet; all I did know was I always felt so alone. Pain is so isolating. It separates us from our friends and family and unable to understand what we struggle with. It creates a silent wedge. A barrier we put up to protect ourselves, both physically and emotionally. It's very lonely.

Now don't get me wrong. I wouldn't want you to understand. I don't wish this suffering on my worst enemy, but until you walk it, you can't talk it.

People line up to give you inspiring words of wisdom or tell you to work more or distract yourself, but unless your saddled with the pain yourself, you don't get a real say on the topic.

This realization on how alone I felt inspired me. It excited me! It gave me hope! Hope that I could share my story and my journey, and it could be my road map to healing my heart. Hope that putting myself and my suffering out there to the world could help even one person who was in my shoes.

Boosted with Rachel Hollis's confidence, I went out to the field by my house and recorded my first take, then a second, then a third, then a twentieth. It took me so long to be able to articulate my journey, how real the lows were and how far I had come already, even if sometimes I didn't recognize it. Finally, it felt ready. As I walked the quick joint back to my house, I noticed the day had passed. Something strange happens when you are nervous, time goes faster.

It seems to quicken with your increased heartbeat. Well, mine must have been pumping a mile a minute at a rate that would have cardiologists standing by with paddles to shock me back to reality.

Shaking like a leaf, I counted to three, took a big sip of my white haven Sav Blanc, and hit post.

The result of my three seconds of bravery blew my mind. Within the first twenty-four hours, I had hundreds of responses. People who had no idea I suffered with pain, and I really never felt like I suffered silently. People opened up and shared their pain story with me.

It blew my mind! I realized then that we don't really share or talk about our pain. I think we feel, at least in my experience, it somehow makes us weaker or maybe we aren't as strong, mentally or physically, as we once had thought. This experience made me realize that is a total load of crap, excuse my language. Just saying it's not true, didn't seem big enough. I think if you get up every day, take on the world, feed your kids, clean your house, see your friends, or whatever your life looks like, all while in pain, that that makes you even stronger.

I believe that just because we can suffer silently doesn't mean we should. That idea cultivated in my brain. I wanted to create a community and a safe space for those suffering, to suffer together instead of suffering alone. I wanted to spread the word that "it's okay to be in pain," or that "it's all right to 'not be all right.'" I wanted to bring chronic pain out of the shadows. I wanted take it away from being a dirty little secret and make it something that is celebrated as a part of our strength and part of our story. That's when "#Pain2" was born. A million days in pain together is easier than a single day in pain alone.

Fueled with that purpose, I soldiered on with the blog. My goal was to affect one person, to have my story change a single person's outlook on the daily struggles of what's pain truly is: "For anyone else sitting on the bathroom floor with bottle in hand as I had been."

One day, while mindlessly scrolling through Facebook, I came across an ad for a TEDx—a bundle of people getting together to share their stories and journeys—sounded right up my alley. Align with my new quest, I clicked on the link. As I scrolled down the page, using the old-school mouse that still had the textured clicking—you remember the kind from elementary-school computer's class, where every scroll bubbled below your pointer finger, yeah that one. Clearly in need of updating my technology—suddenly, my finger came to a stop. It stopped almost before my brain registered why. In front of my eyes was a large orange button. Now this was no ordinary button; this was the button I had been waiting my whole life for. This was the button that would change my life as I knew it.

"Apply to be a speaker," how could I resist. A chance to take my blog further, help more people, and share my story on a huge platform. Um… Yes, please! As I began feverishly filling in the information page, I couldn't help but laugh at my gumption. What did I really have to offer such a prestigious name of speakers? I knew I wouldn't be chosen, but this was the kick in the rear I needed to motivate myself to take the next steps in my "#Pain2" journey. As I came to the button on the bottom of the page, I hesitated. All filled in, but there was one step left: submitting it. Ten, fifteen, then twenty seconds went by. My finger lay motionless on the mouse pad. I was actively willing it to move, for my finger to be brave enough for my whole body. One second of courage and one finger was all this would take to be off and away. Click! It was gone. Too late to chicken out now. Too late to take it all back! Although I knew this was more a metaphorical step, as it was only meant to motivate me to expand my goals, I was elated. As I danced around my bed-room, still holding the glass of liquid courage I had so desperately needed, I couldn't help but beam. A little part of me, one I wasn't willing to admit to the world, thought this could be it.

*****

Three days, seven hours, and thirty minutes after my TEDx application was sent off, my phone rang. A 732 area code—oh joy, I must have won a cruise or some raffle I never entered. They only needed my credit card to hold the spot (insert eye roll here). As I answered the phone, all set to tell off the scammer on the other line, my heart stopped. This was no spam call; it was my first round interview for the TEDx position.

Having just had such an emotional 180 degrees from annoyed to speechless, it took me a noticeable pause to speak when they asked the first round of questions. *How are they calling? I have no speaking experience. I am new to my cause and seriously... I'm just a barn girl... Who cares.* In my world, that is a dime a dozen. Well, apparently, not in every circle. Apparently, there is a whole world of people out living life, not concerned about the next competition; their horse's feet schedule, when the next jump school was, or how to bubble wrap them into not hurting themselves. Apparently, lots of people cared. My first interview flew by. I found my voice and excitedly rattled off answers as if the woman on the other line and I went way back.

As the interview came to a close, I was shocked to learn they had had over three hundred applicants, and no, they weren't calling them all as I had first suspected.

The first interview quickly led to a second and third. Every time the next step came, I was shocked. Then, after all three interviews, nothing. Radio silence for a whole week. I mean, I understood not being selected, but all the inter-views had allowed a little hope to creep in. Hope that, perhaps, my story was worth something. That people did care, and they were interested.

After a disappointing realization that I didn't get the spot, an email popped up on my phone. I can still remember the sound of the alert. I had, in anticipation, set my alert to a cheery and hopeful song. "Build Me Up Buttercup" by The Foundations chimed away on my phone. I couldn't help but bounce along as I opened the email. I defy you to listen to those uplifting lyrics and not get at least a foot tap going.

I screamed. I yelled so loud, at a pitch only dogs could hear. Thinking I had, perhaps, just been murdered in some gruesome home invasion; my husband sprinted up the stairs from his "man cave," to my happy dance.

To give you an accurate visual, do you remember *The Ugly Truth*, with Katherine Heigel? You know, her excited "Spazzy dance," yeah, it was something like that. Not the sophisticated dance I would rock out in front of anyone, for sure. But the emotions took hold, and it was no holds barred of the dance moves.

Knowing nothing of what was causing my seizure like moves and the shrieking, I was physically restrained until I could use grown-up words. All I could muster, half from excitement and half from being completely out of breath, was "I'M IN!" as if somehow those two words made sense with no context.

The TEDx was scheduled for September, so I had four months to craft my perfect talk.

A thousand and one drafts filled the trash bin as I struggled to find the words to describe the journey I had just narrowly survived. How could I stand in front of two hundred people and share in great detail the story of how I fought, for two years, not to end my life.

Nothing I would draft seemed strong enough or impactful enough to help someone else in real struggles.

Months of rewrites and still nothing. Coming closer and closer to the deadline, my worry sank in. It is that kind of self-doubt that can rattle a person to their very core. *What if I am not good enough? What if my story isn't impactful enough? What if I forget my speech and stand up there like a total dummy?* But the greatest worry of all was, *What if I wasn't meant to do this?* I had justified the accident as a part of my journey, leading me to speaking. Everything happening like a set of dominos slowly dropping along onto the next piece until they fully collapsed to reveal the full picture that had been hidden from sight.

All this negative self-banter continued until the universe stepped in. At Shoppers Drug Mart, picking up a prescription for an antibiotic I was in need of, a beautiful brunette woman lurked around the corner of isle 4, staring at me. Everywhere I went, she followed close behind, still gawking.

Did I have something in my teeth? Had I unknowingly cut her off in the parking lot? Was she waiting for the perfect moment to exact her revenge?

Finally, after twenty minutes of this strange case of stalking, I turned abruptly around to face her, made full eye contact, and boldly asked, "Do I know you?"

Startled by my change in stance, the woman shook her head yes, then no.

So which one is it?

Nervously, after being discovered for an almost criminal case of stalking, she quickly stated, "You don't know me, but you're Kat. I know you."

What was this? A riddle?

The confused look of my face, coupled with the blond hair that already makes me look lost on the best of days, quickly led her to expand on her brain twister of an answer.

"I know you from your blog. I have followed it for a year, and it has saved my life," she stated. She proceeded to tell me her story with chronic pain and how she had survived a nasty battle with breast cancer and now suffered with pain, postchemo. She talked to me about her loss of self, her battle with depression, and the anxiety she was left with would ensure her life would never be the same. Moved to tears, we hugged. Yes, we hugged, both awkwardly crying, in the middle of isle 6 at the drug store.

Her bravely sharing her story and the impact my words and ability to verbalized the pain had literally saved her life. That the raw real videos where I "ugly cry" on camera, showing all the real and raw moments of pain, made her feel less alone.

I got home fully inspired. If I could help someone I didn't even know, I could do this. She was my one—the one person I had set out to help.

The talk that had taken me months, several hundred drafts, and copious amounts of Kim Crawford Sav Blanc to write started to pour out of me. Twenty minutes, and she was done. My masterpiece.

I had been missing the emotion and the vulnerability. I realized that is our life. We all try to put on a brave face, lessen our pain to make others feel more comfortable with it. That is just how I had been writing it. I cringed at the idea of saying, "I wanted to kill myself" in front of two hundred people live, and hundreds more virtually. However, this was my truth. In order for this speech to land and really resonate, I would have to be raw, and I would have to be real. The legacy of my blog depended on it. I had never shied away from being honest and authentic on videos just because, while you are taping, it is just me (and usually my dogs). No one there to make faces or gasps at our reactions. I had been hiding behind my screen for safety, but the training wheels were about to come off.

CHAPTER 9

One Day at a Time

September 17 2019, the big day. I had flown to Nashville the previous week-end with friends for a convention. I arrived home long enough to shower, repack, and kiss my hubby and dogs before jet-setting off to New Brunswick, Canada—a part of the country that feels almost like going back in time.

Our talk was held in a beautiful old fishing town that I couldn't help but be reminded of swallow falls from *Cloudy with a Chance of Meatballs*. Yes, I am a six-year-old at heart.

From the old buildings that had never seen a facelift, to the old school Volkswagen bug made into a cop car, I was enchanted. At one point, we literally witnessed an older woman in an apron chasing a boy down the street while holding her rolling pin, fresh from bakery. Where does that happen in the twenty-first century? I loved it.

My mom and I arrived with one whole day of leisure before the talk, and there was no way that those twenty-four hours would be spent stressing; we had to see this unique, somewhat quirky, little town in its entirety. We walked the seawall and the beautiful parks nearby. We even found ourselves so lost we ended up on a little ferry to nowhere, only to turn around and ferry right back where we had just came from.

Our night finished with one of the most delicious Italian meals I have had to date. I swear I would fly all the way back there just to have that lasagna and sea breeze martini again at Italian by night. Something about the creativity of additive of orange to a classic martini flavor won me over completely.

Eventually, the day could go on no more; it was time for bed. How could one be expected to sleep? The most exciting and arguably important day of my "new life" was tomorrow. After watching all the horrible dateline TV, *Titanic* (yes, I know, longest movie ever), and some random dance parties, my tolerant mother could stay awake no longer. Her eyes fluttered until they could not stay open anymore. As she fell into sleep, I crept out of bed. I sat by the window, looking out at the full moon. It felt like my whole world was waiting for me. No fear, no pressure, just inner peace. A moment of calm before the storm of busy that was to come. For a brief moment, all the trauma of my injury and the pain, both mental and physical, seemed worth it. Like the universe had been playing puppet master the whole time, and I was on some greater path.

*****

Previous to our speech, we had been asked to submit a written copy of our talk, and based on that, the group of organizers had selected me to be their closer, no pressure right.

My amazing mom and lifetime cheerleader made the long trek to come and support me. We rose early and went for a long walk along the wharf to clear any last-minute nerves before sound check. The beautiful scene of the ocean meeting land, while birds danced above, was just what the doctor ordered. That and the half sweet mocha we had managed to acquire at the little bakery next to the hotel. Moving my body by now was my number 1 trick for success to keep my body and mind working harmoniously. A quick stroll, and it was time.

As I arrived on scene for sound check, I was met with a sea of nervous energy waving from person to person. From the team working hard to pull together a fabulous event, to the other speakers waiting for their turn, it was nothing but emotions. One girl was even so nervous she was doing handstands in the speaker's lounge; her personal nerve-busting trick. But not me, I felt a sense of calm. A feeling that only ever hit me before heading down centerline in dressage, like we were meant to be here. Nothing was going to take away this amazing experience, especially not fear.

As my turn finally came to walk the stage in my microphone and practice standing with the lights all on me before the real thing happened, I wanted to cry. In that moment, I knew! I knew this was going to be the pinpoint of change. The event that thrust me into a different life and career. Not only did the universe have a plan for me, but it was leading me down the path to help others. I remember thinking just one! If this speech can reach just one new person, either in person or the live broadcasting, it would all have been worth it. Every day in pain, every moment of feeling hopeless and being lost, all worth it.

As I walked down the slope in the auditorium, past all the chairs, in the dimly lit room with the horrible red velvet-colored carpet, I knew... I have got this! It was an incredible feeling. For the first time, it was more than about me. It was about who I could impact, who would hear this speech and decide like me to put down the bottle of pills and rise up. It became about that one person! And it is so easy to give a speech to one person. That was my focus.

Feeling invigorated, I bounced like a little happy bunny from a kid's cartoon. From sound check back to meeting my mom for a quick bite to eat before the real excitement started, full of anticipation and no nerves, I frolicked into the little restaurant attached to our hotel room.

We had one hour before the real deal started, and a glass of celebration bubbles seemed to be just what the doctor ordered.

A quick sip and back in a flash. Back to the small blank room with no distinguishing art or colors on the walls. The only things in the room were the nervous other speakers and a giant projection screen. They set the screen to allow the other participants of the day to all hear and support each other.

As the nervous little redhead dressed in all black darted in the room, we all went silent. You could have heard a pin drop as she announced the five-minute call for the first speaker. The first speaker, or I should say speakers, were two young men, who had organized the only joint speech of the day.

As we all watched in anticipation, the walked to the stage, across the slope, down the horrible red carpet, up the three wooden steps, and into the spotlight, out of some sort of solidarity, to the other speakers we didn't even know, no one even took a breath. Finally, they began their speech.

The speech flew by until, right in the middle, they got lost in their placement and messed up. Wait, that had never occurred to me. *What if I forget!*

They pulled an amazing recovery, but then speaker after speaker fumbled. One girl actually had to ask the audience for a moment to recover her thoughts. Okay now I'm really nervous. Most of these people were professionals or industry leaders.

As speaker by speaker left to face the music, I began to pace. Not out of nerves, but out of sheer hope. Hope that I can do my topic justice, that I won't get in my own way, that I can stay authentically me and reach that one person.

Finally, no one left waiting in the room, and it was my turn to close off the night. As I walked, for the second time that day down the red carpet, I couldn't help feeling like this was my red-carpet moment. That I, in that moment, was

Blake Lively at the Oscars or heading to a big movie premier. This was the moment. Now find me one person to help!

As the speech began, I struggled to regain my breath. Having your name announced in front of hundreds is a staggering feeling that I'm not sure I will ever fully get used to. To be honest, I hope it never loses its affect. It's a powerful feeling, and after the years in pain, the loss of identity and faith in myself filled me with pride. The same pride I once felt when they announced as I would enter an arena for competition, "And riding for Canada, Kat Naud."

The speech flew by, with gasps at the photos that accompanied my description of my fall, and tears as I explained the turmoil my life had gone through. As I talked on and on through the journey my life had taken and the steps it took to fight my way back to some resemblance of myself, I found my strid— really feeling the words and the connection they were having to my audience. When it was finally through, I had my first standing ovation—a moment that will be engraved in my head and heart for all the rest of my days.

This amazing experience had come to a close, and it was time to rejoin my normal life. But what did that look like now? In my head, I was still a barn girl searching for a new direction, but in my heart, I was a speaker. Every day began with this new sort of turmoil. Finding a way to amalgamate the world I had come from with the life I wanted for my future. The how to do it was simple: *one day at a time!*

That's all any of us can really handle in pain. One day at a time. Or if it's really hard, one hour at a time, or one task at a time. I knew if I wanted to keep the ball rolling on this idealistic future of speaking, I had to walk the walk. But what did that really look like?

It looked like hard work getting up each day to write, to blog, post, and to inspire.

Now horses and the barn family I have spent years cultivating will always be a huge part of my life and my heart, but it was time to take a step back, to give myself the space and time to grow in this new direction, and it was also time to be honest with myself about my love of sport.

Three-day eventing had been my heart and soul for twenty-plus years, but it wasn't anymore. I lived with the repercussions of the dangers of our sport. I spent, and will spend, every day in pain. How could I, in good conscience, send children out on course with that kind of doubt in my head. The short answer, I couldn't. It was time to move my event students over to another coach, take a step back from full-time teaching, and run the family business. I kept my students who either had interest in jumpers or dressage (two other disciplines of riding) and passed the rest onto my longtime friend and my former coach. I have always prided myself in being true and authentic in my speaking, and it was time to walk that walk in my barn life.

CHAPTER 10

The Greatest Joy

Have you ever heard the expression "bad news comes in threes"? Well, karma must have balanced that out, so good news travels the same way.

Monday morning and back to work after a weekend away, I had spent the whole weekend enjoying the beautiful early spring up at the Shuswap lake, where my husband and I are lucky enough to have a place.

Mondays after a peaceful weekend away always felt so tiresome, but little did I know, this Monday had some twists and turns waiting for me.

After being gone, my amazing staff had run the show for the weekend at the barn. I guess they didn't want to bother me with any questions, so they decided to wait for my return. As I walked in the big metal sliding door to our barn, I was greeted with two anxious girls. "Um, can I borrow you?" Michelle, our barn manager, squeezed out. Now Michelle has done this job, and done it extremely well for many years, so right away, I could recognize on her tone something was happening.

She led me out of the barn and to the back paddocks. Now Michelle is not one of the tallest of girls, but you would never know that today, her shorter legs taking the whole barn in what seemed to be just a few strides.

I hurried after her. *Oh god, what now?* I thought. *Mondays!*

As we approached the paddock of a palomino pony named Luna (Luna was one of our regular lesson ponies; her hair shone golden blond and almost reflected in the sun), she reminded all the little ones that came around of spirit from the animated cartoon. She was a beautiful mare but had always been on the, well, rather large side width-wise. Some would say fat, but we don't fat shame. We had, for months, been actively trying to put her on a "Jenny Craig" diet for fear of her health. It's not health for any of us to carry lots of extra weight but especially a pony; it made them more susceptible to a condition called founder, which could be deadly.

Months of this so-called diet and no improvement. I sneakily suspected the lesson kids have been overtreating her again.

That is until Michelle, in the most unconfident voice, ever asked me, "Is she pregnant?"

I scoffed. There was no way. We have had her for five months and don't own a stallion.

But to not dismiss Michelle's question, I gave the little golden pony a once-over. All around, she seemed chubby and round, nothing new to us having her, but then as I took a pity glance under her belly to be sure, I was speechless.

SHE WAS! And not only that, but she was, far along. This little mare was about a week or two from becoming a momma. She was already what we call bagged up, meaning she was filling with milk in preparation for her upcoming baby. Surprise number 1!

I leapt into gear; we were months behind on planning and prepping. Vets called, straw bales ordered, and oh yeah, I should call the co-owner, who just happened to be my mom. As I dialed the all-too-familiar number that hadn't change since I was in the fourth grade, I was met with even more excitement on the phone. I couldn't even get a word in edgewise. They had just bought a puppy! A new addition to our four-legged family for the second time that day. Surprise number 2!

Finally, after hearing all the excited details of the new puppy, like breed, color, age, and when she would be set to arrive, I interrupted with my own four-legged arrival story. She was just as blown away as I was. My mom, who I don't think has ever been speechless, was at a loss for words. I quickly decided this conversation needed more than an electronic device and hung up and made my way back through the barn and into the parking lot, adjacent to her house. As the big glass door opened, I was met with "WHAT" a hundred times. There were no real words to describe a surprise foal.

As we both sat in the kitchen at the long marble bar setting, no one spoke, both in such shock about what was to come.

It was one of those unseasonable hot spring days, and I was waiting on the vet, so figured why not wait in the cool comfort of the shade from the kitchen. Now if you have ever been in double shock, you will know that awkward self-silence you sit in. The kind where even your inner monologue takes a lunch break. That where I was…total mental moment. All of a sudden, a pulsating feeling shocked me back to reality. My phone was going off, buzzing to warn me of an incoming text. That is when surprise number 3 came—the greatest surprise I have ever had, to date. Now that is saying a lot. When I turned nineteen, my mom surprised me by flying my best friend in from out of province and hid him under a large wrapped box. I am not even sure if she gave him air holes as that could have ruined the surprise. Or my twenty-first birthday, when I was whisked off to Vegas with two of my best friends, all orchestrated by my amazing mom again, all that is to say is I have had some incredible surprises in my life, but this one takes that cake.

Brianna, the young rider who had purchased Jackson, wanted to inform me she was retiring him from upper-level eventing at the end of that season and wasn't able to keep him. Did I want him to come home and retire with me? YES! It had been five years since I had seen Jackson, and the idea of him coming home made my heart soar.

Tears flooded my face as if a faucet had been turned on behind my eyes. Happy tears and sounds escaped my body without control. I had dreamt of this day for the last five years, and it was really coming true.

The horse I had loved for fifteen years was coming home to me.

*****

The big day! Months and months of almost patiently waiting finally arrived. My boy was coming home. As the large professional shipping and hauling trailer barreled into the parking lot, the ground shook. It seemed to shake in sync with my anticipation. They decided to fully back up and turn around before coming to a stop to unload. It took every ounce of self-control I had to not yell at that to stop! Just stop and let me have my horse, then you can do whatever you want. After I had Jackson in my arms, they could do donuts in the parking lot for all I cared. I waited, kept my mouth closed, and gripped my fists tighter. It was all I could do to keep myself from leaping at the trailer in motion.

When they finally parked and turned the engine off, I didn't wait, I didn't stop to introduce myself to the hauler, or even say hello for that matter. I had way better things to get to.

I flung the heavy metal ramp down, a feat of strength that usually takes two full-grown people to accomplish, but I didn't care. I was the mom lifting the car to get to her kid trapped below. Nothing was slowing me down.

As I sprinted up the ramp into the six horse head-to-head trailer, I was met with a familiar sound. Jackson's nicker.

He recognized me! After these five years apart, who knew exactly who I was after just a glance. Everything slowed down. My heart was finally full again. Calmly, I unsnapped the cold metal tie in the trailer as I simultaneously clipped his yellow lead rope to the bottom ring of his halter. He hasn't worn this rope since the last day we saw each other. We peacefully unloaded from the trailer as two old friends together again.

Standing in the parking lot, I collapsed into him. Both my arms spreading the width of his broad shoulders and up to the top of his neck. The horse version of a bear hug. Many of my close friends and barn family had come out that day to welcome this handsome prince home. There, surrounded by my loved ones, we stood, frozen in our embrace. The horse, that's name was tattooed not only on my shoulder, but in my heart, had come home forever.

CHAPTER 11

Not Better Pain but Better Brain

So what does it truly mean to be on the other side of chronic pain? Does it mean your magically pain-free? I hope so, but that hasn't been my journey. My pain will be my life's companion, but I have acquired some amazing tricks and tools to help combat the pain. I say all the time to my blog followers, "It's not better pain but better brain." But what does that really mean?

Well, here are my steps, stages, and what I have learned through a plethora of trial and error.

Let's start with the basics:_*the stages of pain.*

Now we have all heard of the stages of grief, but chronic pain has its own stages as well. They follow a similar pattern but with some distinct twists. It makes sense that they would be similar since you really are grieving a loss, the loss of yourself before the pain. That's actually one of the hardest steps: acceptance.

Denial

This step was at least, in my opinion, the one that was really easy to get stuck on. For admitting my pain was really meant more than just being in pain for the rest of my life. The denial stage is such a sweet comfort zone to start your journey. It means we are blissfully unaware, at least we are letting ourselves be unaware, that everything might not return to normal.

Everyone will experience pain in their life, from a broken arm or sprained ankle or perhaps recovering from a surgery, all very unpleasant, but all recoverable. The difference between pain and chronic pain is the duration of suffering. Chronic pain is pain lasting longer than six months.

Now why denial is so easy to get stuck in, at least for me, is because I was no stranger to injury or pain. I had fallen before and was sure I would again. Occupational hazard, I guess. It's easy and tempting to stay in this place, to stay in the sweet spot of temporary pain. Now that might sound odd. Sweet spot of pain? How the heck can pain be sweet? Well, as you read above, it's not till you lose hope that things become harder. Temporary injuries are full of hope, full of short-time frames and counting down the days till you can take your fully autographed cast off and reveal the fresh-healed arm below.

Denial will end; mine was with a bang. A doctor ripping my hope away, but yours might look different. A slow realization that you aren't progressing, that seasons are passing and your pain and body seem stagnant, like a pond that hasn't seen wild life in a decade. I'm here to tell you, "THAT'S OKAY!" In fact, if your leaving denial, you are on the road to mental and physical recovery. No one can heal from chronic pain in the denial stage.

In denial, we aren't ready to address the issue at hand: that we need more help, more time, and most importantly, more resources to combat the struggles that are ahead. It would be like standing at base camp of Everest, thinking, *What a nice gentle hike I am about to embark on*. Not realistic. As you stare up at that behemoth of a mountain, you need to be mentally prepared. Ready to go into battle, so to speak. *So* put on your armor, and let's get to fighting.

Bargaining

Now this is where things mix up a little, at least for me. Bargaining came before anger. It wasn't bargaining with some higher power or praying to "insert your religion here," but with myself. Okay, if I can get out of bed today, I get to have a nap this afternoon, or if I just force myself to the gym, I don't have to go tomorrow. Or if I could only ride my horse today, tomorrow I will take it easy on my body. But here is the problem with that way of thinking: You are spending tomorrows spoons today. And when you borrow something from tomorrow, not only do you owe back pay, but you are starting the next day off in a deficit.

I spent months in this place, feeling good one day, so massively overdoing it, always wanting to push the envelope and have some feelings of normalcy, only to suffer for in the following days.

If I'm being really honest, it was like a yo-yo.

You know those fad diets your friends have been on. Where they are super strict with themselves and lose ten pounds only to find it, and usually more, a few weeks later? Well, that was me with my activity.

It took me months to learn to regulate, to learn "little and often" instead of "superhero" to "couch potato." It is a lesson I hope you can read here and learn without needing the highs and lows I struggled with. Now the physical toll of this was brutal and crippling, but the emotional toll was much more substantial.

Going from days of feeling like "myself," or at least my previous self, to feeling like Sid the Sloth from *Ice Age* would give me the kind of emotional swings I could only assume bipolar people have.

All these emotional highs and lows led me back down the rabbit hole to the next stage.

Depression

Depression hit me like a ton of bricks. Jackson landing on me from 550 meters per minute on top of me hit less dramatically less than the depression. You can run and run from it, but as soon as you stop moving, it catches up to you. Well, it did! And I didn't just have a little drizzle; I was caught in hurricane Kat. My own personal monsoon dumping its pain, sorrow, and all the feelings I had repressed, down onto me like a ton of bricks. What I can tell you about my battle with depression is *ask for help!* This took me a long time, too long in fact. Suffering alone and silently is *not* okay. This does not make you weak, nor does it make you less than or pathetic. And perhaps you are reading this thinking, *Of course it doesn't*, then good for you. You are ahead of the curve. I grew up thinking mental health was a sign of weakness, something that could be solved by working harder, distracting myself more or just keeping myself busy. Now don't get me wrong, it's so important to try to keep living; it's okay to not be okay. It's okay to need a little help, but here is the kicker, you have to pull up your big-girl panties and ask for the help. If you are not comfortable talking to anyone in your life, see someone else.

There are hundreds of amazing professionals with the whole job description to be judgment free and listen to you.

Not into being shrunk? Tell one person. Just one. Someone in your life that makes you feel safe. They can be your emergency contact for depression. Someone you can text even a damn emoji too that is like a bat signal for needing help or support. Just one!

I am going to write this, and I hope to my very core you hear me; it is okay to need help. Let me say that again so you really could hear me, "*It's okay* to need help!" In fact, it is human. It is the human condition to crave and need interaction with others, and when you are depressed, that's the first thing to go. We isolate ourselves to lick our emotional wounds in private, but that is the worst possible solution. Reach out, be heard, and know that this phase, although the hardest, can and will get better, so do not quit on yourself. Your physical pain, or even emotional pain, might be permanent, but this stage doesn't have to be. Hang in there, my friend.

Anger

Now, everyone suffering in pain knows this stage all too well. Being mad as hell. Let me tell you, that's normal and it's okay. It's okay to be infuriated or frustrated—frustrated with your situation or even, in my case, with my body. A thought that percolated constantly with me was, *How could I not heal? I am only twenty-five.* Surely, a quarter century was still a baby in the grand scheme of life. My body owed me that much, didn't it? You are not guaranteed anything in life, and health is one of those scary unknown. Something we take for granted until it's gone. If your reading this and you are healthy and happy, thank your lucky stars and appreciate it every damn day. And if you're not, it's okay to feel cheated. What is not okay, and something I totally did wrong, is to steamroll your frustrations onto the people you are closest to.

I dumped my moods onto those who I trusted and knew would still be there even with these unfair emotional intrusions. Looking back, it's one of my biggest regrets. I wish I had been emotionally sound, or at the very least, aware enough to recognize what I was doing.

I guess hindsight is twenty-twenty. Something that really helped me combat this was a punching bag. Literally! I joined a little women's boxing group, and although I was useless as a bump on a log, it helped me have a safe and healthy outlet for the anger that felt like it was literally boiling under my skin.

Acceptance/Grieving

This step is such sweet serenity when you finally find it. Like anything worth having, it's a lot of work, fully packed with emotional heavy lifting. My acceptance, or lack thereof, was so tied to me emotionally. Accepting the loss of who I was, the loss of the professional athlete on track to the Olympics, the loss of the girl who could ride ten horses in a day and still have the physical energy and ability to go for a ten-kilometer run after, she was gone; that part of me died that day on the field, and I hadn't really been ready to let her go.

I spent so long stuck in anger with bouts of dissociation that I hadn't let myself realize she was gone. When I began to unpack the boxes of emotions, it was like going through a deceased loved one's belongings for the first time. I was shattered. I bounced back through the stages a million times—denial, anger, denial, and anger all over again.

The one piece that really made this survivable for me was looking for the silver lining. Yes, such a cliché thing to say, but it's true. Everything bad that happens in your life has a bright side. Something that came from the darkness. A loss of a loved one? Perhaps it forced you to reconcile with another family through the passing. Or having your heart broke perhaps helped you find an inner strength and a backbone you didn't know you could muster up. As hard as it is, there is always a bright light from the dark. It might feel impossible to find when you are in the thick of it, like the very start of a long, long tunnel, where the light looks like a speck at the end of the black, but it's there. Go find it!

Mine came though expressing my journey. Through sharing my pain and suffering, I found my community. I found my new "why"—the new thing driving me out of bed. The desire to help that one was greater than the desire to wallow. They say helping others is the greatest way to help yourself, and truer words have never been spoken.

As I began to unpack the bigger why, the little pieces of good started to become clearer to me as well. If I hadn't had my injury, I would have been too swept up in competing to really give my now husband a fair fighting chance for my heart. If I didn't fall, I wouldn't have sold Jackson, which helped me buy the amazing house I am currently writing from. If I hadn't fallen, I wouldn't have had a window into the people who were in my corner—not just friends, but deeply "there for you people." The bend-over-backward-to-be-there-for-you kinda people that we all really need to survive. Hard times have a way of weaning out the fake friends. It's such an important step to know who those thick-and-thin people are in your life, and sometimes it surprises you. It helps you assess your emotional boundaries and prioritize where you put your energy. After all, you have much less of it to give when you live with pain. And lastly, and most importantly, it helped me find a life! A life outside of horses. It gave me balance and a whole full-figured life. It's the difference between sipping on grape juice versus the first sip of a full-bodied red wine. I know I'm more of a white wine girl, but the reference holds.

I hope my journey can help inspire you if you are in the thick of the pain. No matter where you are in your journey with pain, whether emotional or physical or like me, both, keep fighting. There is another side to chronic pain.

It's not pain-free, it's better emotional control of your pain. It's learning and practicing perceiving your pain differently. I will be in pain for the rest of my life, but the same pain that used to be earth-shattering, life-ending pain, now is something I can sit with. It's something I can control, and it's something, through working the steps and moving my body regularly, evenly and consistently, I can manage.

Having been the girl on the bathroom floor with the bottle of painkillers to now, I will say this is, for sure, the other side. Keep walking your path; your journey is just beginning.

Thank you for reading till now. If your still with me, that means, at least I hope, that something about my journey resonated with you. My sincerest hopes for this book and the whole pain journey is to help just one person know they can make it to the other side of chronic pain.

ABOUT THE AUTHOR

Kat has been an international equestrian athlete since a very young age and grew up on a ten-acre equestrian family farm in Surrey, British Columbia.

She is a certified competition coach, an A-level pony club rider, and the owner of a thriving equestrian barn located in Canada.

Kat has taken the serious impacts of her injuries and turned it into an outlet to help inspire others battling chronic pain.

She has done a TEDx talk in New Brunswick and has a pain management blog that has been read around the world.

Printed in the USA
CPSIA information can be obtained
at www.ICGtesting.com
LVHW090742100624
782786LV00006B/132

9 781637 108482